Of pleasant waters, tall buildings and myriad diversions. A place called

Chicago

Unique CityScenes

Distributed by Photoscapes™
565 Drexel Avenue
Glencoe, Illinois 60022
Phone (708) 835-2941

"City of Chicago"

The Near North Side And North Avenue Beach.

CHICAGO

The Chicago of the '90s is vibrant with growth...beautiful in its diversity of architecture...dynamic in its ethnicity...and blessed as always with a clean, blue, bountiful lake that shapes the city's character. Indeed without Lake Michigan's proximity, Chicago might just as well have been St. Louis or Indianapolis.

The downtown skyline which can be seen from any number of private and public cruise ships is surely a wonder of the urban world...and the rest of the town ain't bad either. Sure, Chicago battles poor and aging neighborhoods like any big city. But nowadays it wins more than it loses. Recent decades have seen the end of a population outflow to the suburbs. Today, central neighborhoods like River North are defying the conventional wisdom of a generation ago and proving you don't need old apartment buildings to renovate or replace. *Any* kind of funky old structure will do. Today's relentless urban "rehabber" stops at nothing. Snugged up against the Chicago River's unattractive north branch was seedy Clybourn Avenue, just about the dreariest collection of warehouses, saloons, and whatnot you could imagine. We're talking mid-'80's here. Today, it's the super-glitzy "Clybourn Corridor" with marvelous restaurants, trendy shops, and thousands of young enthusiastic new residents who couldn't imagine a better neighborhood in a city anywhere.

The pattern is being repeated elsewhere, particularly around the Loop, Chicago's downtown core, as renewal pushes outward. Yet the Loop itself remains the focus of Chicago. New skyscrapers are to be seen from South Wacker Drive all the way north to Michigan Avenue which has become an international wonderland of shopping, compared by some to Hollywood's fabled Rodeo Drive. If you have money to spend, the chic merchants on North Michigan will make spending it a pleasure. Rivaling the traditional State Street Shopping Zone, particularly for milady's clothing dollar, Michigan Avenue offers Saks, Marshall Field, Lord and Taylor, Nieman Marcus, Bloomingdale's, and scores of smaller boutiques to tempt the shopper. Fronted on the north by the venerable Drake Hotel - Queen Victoria would have liked it - and anchored on the south by the still dazzling Wrigley Building with its suggestion of Seville's Giralda Tower, the Avenue beckons visitor and resident alike to its commercial delights.

Chicago's stunning downtown lake front is guarded by Grant Park which, from Randolph Street to Roosevelt Road, says "no buildings east of Michigan Avenue," a legacy of famed urban planner Daniel Burnham.

Continued on page 16

The sun rises over a beautiful skyline.

Aerial view of the United Center. Home of the Bulls and Blackhawks.

East view from Burnham Park Harbor.

Sears Tower - the World's Tallest Building

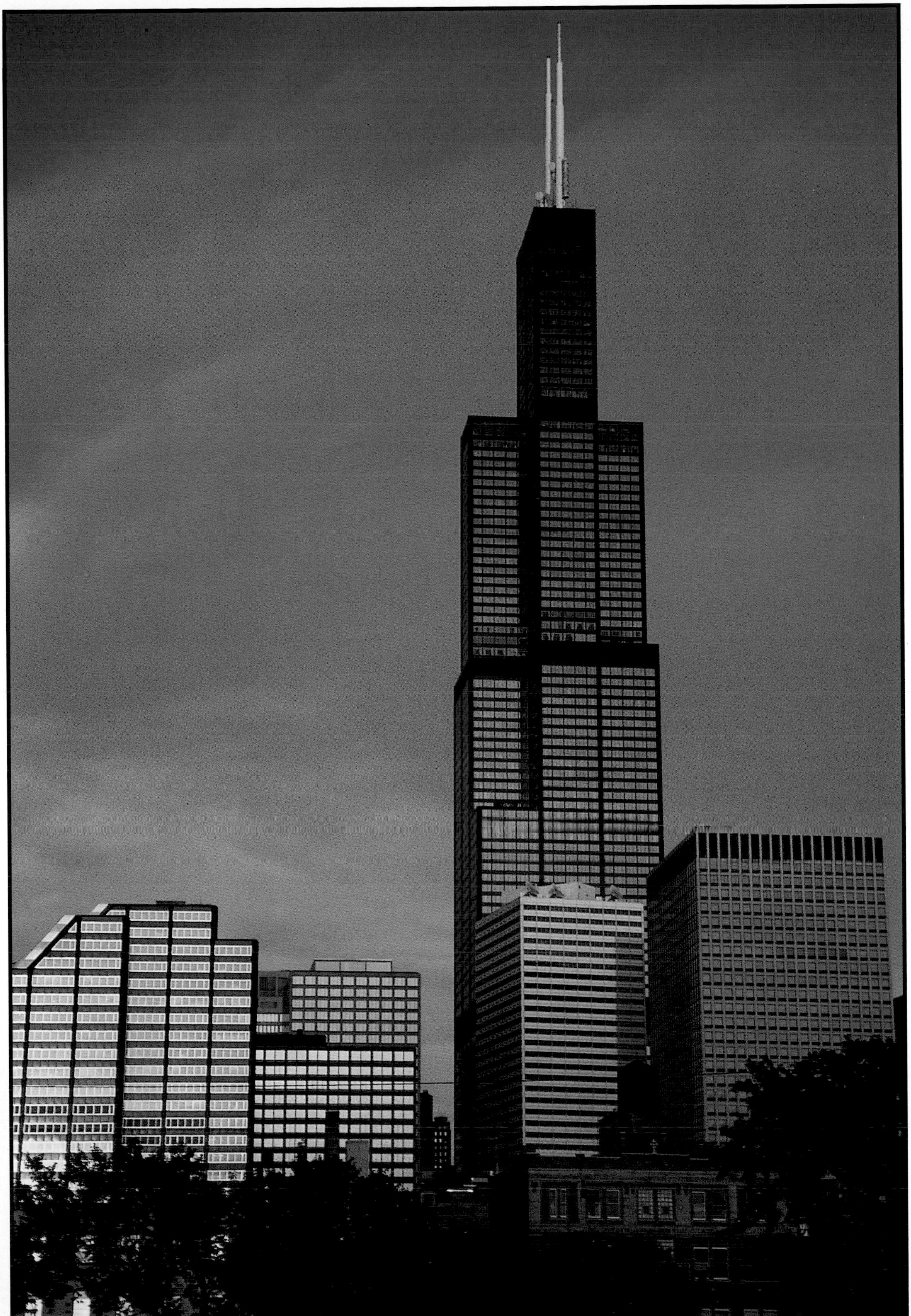

"Taller than the Clouds."

Sears Tower on Wacker Drive.

Sears Tower

Westward over the "Prairie".

Looking north.

Spectacular! Chicago Harbor with *two* yacht clubs - one is actually on a boat (a large boat). Gardens, athletic fields, tennis courts. And the jewel in the crown - the Petrillo Music Shell offering open air free summer concerts by the Grant Park Symphony Orchestra and much more. World class jazz and blues festivals...a growing folk music agenda...and pop music events of all kinds.

Grant Park is host to "Taste Of Chicago" in late June which has become a solid hit both for people who live here and people who are passing through. "Taste " is today what folks in the '60's used to call a "happening". More than a hundred Chicago restaurants set up booths along Columbus Drive offering every imaginable kind of food. And don't think for a minute that this is out-of-doors picnic foodstuff. You'll find each purveyor putting his or her best foot forward, for "Taste" is not only supposed to ring up a sturdy short term profit, it's also meant to create lasting friendships with the locals as dining out becomes more and more a way of life. Local radio stations broadcast from booths at "Taste", and concerts abound at the Music Shell. It's all very exciting and quite the place to be.

"Taste" ends just in time for the city's single biggest blowout - the July 3rd pre-Independence Day "loudenboomer" in Grant Park. Over a hundred thousand people (estimates vary widely) gather around the music shell to hear the orchestra deliver a rousing concert climaxed by the "1812 Overture" by Tchaikovsky complete with bells and all kinds of commotion. One wonders how that particular music ties in with America's Independence Day, but the crowd's enthusiasm sweeps away such niggling doubts. And the ensuing fireworks are really quite beyond description. (Getting home in that crowd has, however, been described very colorfully.) Nobody looks out on the lake, but if they did they'd see hundreds of tiny lights - white ones, green ones and red ones - scattered through the eastern darkness. Boaters from as far away as Waukegan on the north and Michigan City, Indiana, anchor offshore to enjoy the display.

The south end of the park offers several opportunities to learn more about our world: the Field Museum of Natural History, the Shedd Aquarium with its new oceanarium, housing a family of beluga whales, and out on the point the fascinating Adler Planetarium.

The new Harold Washington Library crowns the near south Loop development drive. The building was chosen from several designs submitted in an international competition. Set adjacent to an invigorating assortment of condominium developments and some truly fine restaurants, the neighborhood is solidly on the upward trend.

The Loop - Helicopter view from the south.

Continued on page 36

17

"*The Four Seasons*" *by Marc Chagall.*

"*Flamingo*" *by Alexander Calder.*

The Picasso Statue with hat only
when the Cubs are winning.

Loop architecture as seen from the north branch of the Chicago River.

The Chicago River Bend
Reflections of Wolf Point in the 333 North Wacker Building.

State of Illinois Center: The government embraces modern art

Henri Dubuffet (Sculptor).

and architecture.

Helmut Jahn (Architect).

Prairie Garden in Grant Park

A look across the wildflowers toward Michigan Avenue.

The Garden of the Art Institute

Two lions guarding the Michigan Avenue entrance to the Art Institute of Chicago.

The winning bears celebrating with the lions.

The Annual Mackinac Cup Race.

The fountain lights up at night in ever changing colors.

Buckingham Fountain in Grant Park.

West and north of the Loop, the Chicago River gets cleaner and cleaner. It will, however, be a while before the fond hope of the late Mayor Richard J. Daley is realized. (He envisioned a day when office workers could go down to the river and catch fish at lunchtime and have them cleaned and cooked on the spot).

The southwest riverside attraction is River City, an apartment complex displaying strong echoes of Marina City (Bertrand Goldberg designed them both), once as much a symbol of Chicago as Sears Tower is today. The north and east reaches of the river showcase several distinctive new office buildings and hotels and, of all things, the old broken down forgotten ugly North Pier Terminal has been *transformed* into a multi-use playground and is already a major attraction to visitors. One very loud disco and several enticing restaurants ranging from very casual to very white tablecloth share space with intriguing shops, galleries, at least one museum, and a miniature golf course that lets you play all over town. North Pier is a hit (you can even park your boat), and the north riverfront to the east is being developed into one of the city's most beautiful highrise clusters.

A couple of blocks north is Ontario Street, which has risen from relative obscurity to become the focus of Chicago's trendy restaurant industry. No less than 30 eateries are in place between the lake and the river's north branch, most of them only a few years old. When in doubt, a trip down Ontario Street will stimulate the most jaded appetite. Less expensive and more varied are restaurants on north Halsted Street, itself "rehabbed" up from squalor in the past couple of decades. The segment from North Avenue to Belmont and beyond yields an intriguing mix of seafood specialists and ethnics from middle European to middle Eastern. Chinatown, Little Italy, and Greektown abound with good restaurants of obvious origin. There are half a dozen or so quite fine French restaurants in the city and suburbs, but being possessed of traditional Gallic independence they tend not to cluster; you have to seek them out.

To some people (generally male) the measure of a city can be the number and quality of its professional sports teams. Here, Chicago is richly blessed. The city is represented in all major categories; baseball (two teams), football, basketball, and hockey, and the teams generally do very well. Old timers shake their heads, knowing it can't last, that the misery of losing teams will undoubtedly return.

The Chicago Symphony Orchestra, the Art Institute, the Lyric Opera and the Ravinia Festival are all world class and a source of pride to the citizenry. And for theater-goers, Chicago has become a hotbed of live theater.

Continued on page 50

Grant Park home to Chicago's many festivals.

The Blues

Ravinia Festival.

More jazz.

Chicago Museums

Field Museum of Natural History

Grecian temple statues
adorn the Museum of
Science and Industry.

The Museum of Science and Industry showing the Henry Crown
Space Center.

The Adler Planetarium
the Shedd Aquarium

Wrigley Field - Home of the Chicago Cubs and their fans.

Comisky Park - Home of the Chicago White Sox.   43

John Hancock Center

Catching the Gold Coast in its many moods!

Bas-relief on Michigan Avenue Bridge, commemorating the Fort Dearborn Massacre.

The Wrigley Building.

Michigan Avenue - "The Magnificent Mile".

There are actors here who can actually make a living acting. A glance at the weekend section of either major newspaper will reveal a dozen or more professionally mounted productions ranging from the experimental to the comfortably entertaining to the classic. It's a great town for culture vultures.

Ethnic festivals, some in the neighborhoods, some in lakefront parks, and art fairs pop up like mushrooms in the summer. The beaches are free, nicely maintained and scattered generously along the lakefront where harbors aren't. Air and water shows highlight the summer season, and the gaudy "Venetian Night" attracts thousands of onlookers to see the yachts all dressed up and parading in Chicago Harbor.

Yet when all impressions of Chicago are collected, sorted, and sifted, the tall buildings provide the strongest images. The city has representatives of virtually every American architectural trend. Since the great fire of 1871 (survived by the castle-like Water Tower at Chicago and Michigan Avenues), Chicago has never stopped rebuilding. And because bed rock is near the surface, going high, higher, and highest is no great problem.

Frank Lloyd Wright toyed with the idea of a mile high building. Yet his main legacy (much of it in the suburb of Oak Park) is low "prairie style" buildings, most of them private homes. His Robie House is lovingly preserved at the University of Chicago. Wright and his predecessors, Sullivan and Adler, were part of a "school" of Chicago architecture that inspired generations of followers. But the single greatest influence on today's skyline was a German genuis named Ludwig Mies Van Der Rohe.

Mies came to Chicago in the late '30's to teach at what is now the Illinois Institute of Technology. His lean, ornament-free style can be found all over the city; buildings designed by Mies himself and by his many disciples. Previous Chicago architecture tended to be massive and weighty. Decoration was lavish, often including Grecian pillars. Suddenly, as seen through the eyes of Mies, what had once been regarded as graceful and dignified now seemed silly and superfluous. Van Der Rohe's mystic battle cry, "Less is more" was (and is) widely quoted if seldom understood. Today, you'll find Miesian glass and steel offices and apartment buildings throughout the city. The IBM Building and the graceful Lake Point Tower apartments are prominent examples. More recently the bold black strokes of Bruce Graham in the John Hancock Building and the Sears Tower, and the deco/glassed towers of Helmut Jahn are very much in evidence. Jahn's State of Illinois Building is particularly interesting when viewed from *inside* the huge atrium lobby.

Continued on page 58

On the hour, every hour, the new waterarc spans the Chicago River

The Bulls` Celebration.

The Taste of Chicago.

Concerts in Soldier Field.

Old Chicago Water Tower.

The Holiday Season on Michigan Avenue.

The Rainbow Fleet in Burnham Park Harbor

Belmont Harbor, one of many along the Waterfront.

Outside several Loop buildings are works of sculpture by the world's greatest 20th century artists. Henry Dubuffet created the intriguing "Monument With Standing Beast" which greets the State of Illinois workers each morning; you actually can walk *through* it. There's a giant crimson Alexander Calder sculpture in the Federal Building plaza on South Dearborn Street and a colorful mosaic called "Four Seasons" by Marc Chagall in the plaza adjoining the First National Bank. But the grand-daddy (or grand-mommy -- no one is quite sure) of them all is the Picasso statue at the Daley Center Plaza. People come from miles around to look, to marvel, and to speculate. If you do an about face from the Picasso, you'll see an interesting Miro sculpture in a small plaza on the south side of Madison Street.

The bus tours sponsored by the Architectural Center are surely among the most interesting ways to spend a few hours in Chicago. After winding in and around Loop streets, the comfortable cruiser takes you south through the IIT campus, largely designed by Mies, past such curiosities as the stately home of Muhammed Ali, to a walk-through of Robie House which stands in the shadow of Rockefeller Chapel at the University of Chicago. This "chapel" is about as big as churches get out here on the prairie. There is another very striking religious building in the northern suburb of Wilmette. It is the Bahai Temple, a series of soaring geometric patterns in concrete, beautifully landscaped and as fascinating inside as it is outside.

The temple lies at the end of the north channel of one of the world's most interesting engineering projects - the Sanitary District of Chicago - which reversed the flow of the Illinois River. It used to empty into Lake Michigan at a swamp the Indians called "Checagou," (which meant "wild onion"), but it now empties, via an elaborate system of locks and canals, into the Mississippi. The lake, freed from the river's pollution, developed into the sport-fish-filled playground it is today.

And therein is suggested an upbeat conclusion to this narrative. Back in the '60's the beaches of Chicago were ruined with decaying bodies of millions of little fishes, called alewives. The scene was ugly; the smell was worse. What to do? Moving to Cedar Rapids and abandoning Chicago to the rotten piles of fish was not out of the question. Enter the biologists and the ecologists with a wonderful solution. *People* hate alewives! What likes alewives? Answer: salmon like alewives. Salmon - beautiful, silvery, pink-fleshed and delicious salmon were brought in to eat the pesky alewives, and they did and still do. And if you wonder what all those little motor boats are doing on the lake - well, someone has to keep the shoreline safe from salmon.

"Big John" towers over Streeterville.

Sunrise in Winter.

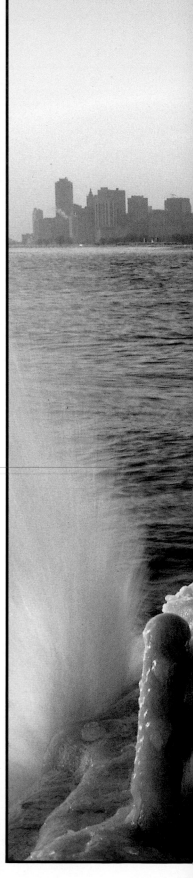

Winter covers the landscape in a blanket of ice and snow.

An aerial panoramic view of Lake Shore Drive looking past the Gold Coast to the North Shore.